\

The Carpenter's Lament in Winter

Poems by

Antoinette Libro

Finishing Line Press
Georgetown, Kentucky

The Carpenter's Lament in Winter

ACKNOWLEDGMENTS

The poems included in this collection have appeared in the following publications, some with slight changes of text or title.

American Writing: A Magazine, "Letter for Virginia" (Fall, 1992).
Dragonfly: A Quarterly of Haiku, "His Old Workshop." (April 1984).
Identity Lessons: An Anthology of Contemporary Writing: "The Last Lesson." (Spring, 2003).
Mad Poet's Review: "Adam's Curse" Vol. 20, 2006.
Paterson Literary Review: "Blueberries in Their Buckets," (2010), "Curtains for Mother," (2013), "Time and Material or, The Carpenter's Lament" (2014), "Filigree," (2015), "Light Hauling" (2015), "Visits Over Time," (2015).
The American Voice in Poetry: The Legacy of Whitman, Williams, and Ginsberg. "Ode to Iris." (2010).
The Aurorean 15th Anniversary Issue: "Dusk," (2010).
The Crafty Poet: A Portable Workshop: "Baggage." (2013).
Wordgathering: A Journal of Disability. "Performance." (Online).
Moonbathing: A Journal of Tanka: "peeling charred skin," or, "Ingredients" Spring/ Summer 2012.

The poems in this collection are fictitious; any resemblance to events or individuals, living or dead, are coincidental, as these works are first and foremost imaginary constructs.

Editor: Christen Kincaid

Cover Art: Louis Braca Jr.

Author Photo: Louis Braca Jr.

Cover Design: Elizabeth Maines

Printed in the USA on acid-free paper.
Order online: www.finishinglinepress.com
also available on amazon.com

Author inquiries and mail orders:
Finishing Line Press
P. O. Box 1626
Georgetown, Kentucky 40324
U. S. A.

Table of Contents

To my Mother and Father

It is necessary to write, if the days are not to slip emptily by.
How else, indeed, to clap the net over the butterfly of the moment?

—Vita Sackville-West, (1892 - 1962) *Twelve Days,* 1928

Ode to Iris

Slowly unfurling
in the garden
teasingly at first
hinting of the
colors to come—

Twelve bearded gentlemen
of royal proportions
arrive, one by one,
nodding in the breeze.

Elegant folds
of blue, lavender, and purple
open into a sea of fleur-de-lis—
while intricate venation
streaks their sleeves.

Twelve bearded gentlemen,
like the twelve apostles
of spring, have come
again, in ruffled Jersey eloquence,
to call on us

In a language
reserved for gods and goddesses—
a language we cannot speak
only admire
from afar.

Blueberries in Their Buckets
(for Elaine)

What is it about this picture
of mother and son
standing in the blueberry fields—

He, the taller of the two,
arm around her shoulder,
her arm around his waist—

Each with a bucket of blueberries
tilted toward the camera
fresh from morning picking.

What is it about this picture
that makes one want to cry?

Perhaps it's the gathering that tells
the story, the gentle nudge that
lets the blueberry fall into your hands

the sheen of silvery blue globes
moist in the early August morning
in the Finger Lakes of New York.

Are their fingers stained with the juice
of the blueberries? What will they do
with them, once home? Have they tasted
he sweetness of the berry already?

What is it about this picture
that makes one want to cry?

The two of them, mother and son,
together in the blueberry fields
in the farmlands of the Finger Lakes—

Fingers stained with blueberries
smiling into the camera
alone with the bounty of the earth and
blueberries in their buckets.

Performance
(for Carol Ann Robertson)

The peach tree in the back yard is three years old—
today peaches the size of marbles dot the branches.

Perhaps this year some of the babies will
mature, blushing with bee-bitten skin.

ripe with the juice of performance.

But, no. Last night gale winds laid the slender tree low
to the ground, roots reaching into air instead of soil.

We spend the morning after righting the tree,
tamping the soil around its roots;

Stronger now than before, perhaps,
 its slim spine loosely tethered to a stake.

Walking back, we pick up a broken branch
and whip the air, then use it as a cane.

Remember the soft sound of her voice,
the matter-of-fact sighs of acceptance

in face of another operation, another rehab.
How she righted herself time after time,

stronger, somehow, more capable than most,
sharing the gifts of expression

on the coffee house platform she created,
where a steady stream

of performers found
their bittersweet voices.

Adam's Curse

We sat together at one summer's end,
That beautiful mild woman, your close friend,
And you and I, and talked of poetry."
    —*Adam's Curse* by W. B. Yeats

One August afternoon
we gather 'round
a great wooden table

in a house on Martha's Vineyard.
Galway sits at the head of the table
with Sharon to his right.

This afternoon he reads Yeats
the 'hollow hearted moon'
in a deep and gravely voice

black hair falling
over his tan forehead
blue eyes downcast.

We listen as the sound
of his voice fills the room
Galway against a wall

of tall paned windows
a bank of green trees
waving in the background.

He reads Yeats in the kind
of voice you'll hear forever
Yeats' beloved poem

of the 'beautiful mild woman,'
and the 'weary-hearted'
just before he finishes

a cardinal flies
into the trees behind him
alighting just above

his right shoulder
bright witness to the rest
of Adam's Curse.

Letter to Virginia
(for Virginia Woolf)

How it must have felt
that cold clear morning in March
walking across the meadows

until you faced the River Ouse—
then finding the heavy stone there
fitting it into your coat pocket.

You abandon your walking
stick on the bank and take that first
step into the waiting river

muddy shoes filling with cold wet
water rising to your knees
encircling your waist, your neck

closing over your head—
your last glimpse of the treetops
askew in the darkening sky.

How it must have been
those last few seconds—
the grip of the cold black

river water delivering
your fierce mind unconscious—
all the demons drowned.

Ingredients

Peeling charred skin
from roasted red peppers
the aroma rises—
in the rosy nectar
memories of mother.

Curtains for Mother

Already on the step ladder
in her 1940s flowered housedress
she is taking down the curtains—
heirloom lace panels, pale silky sheers
or summery dotted Swiss—
the curtains fall into her arms
like a billowing prom dress.
She carries them into the big bathroom
where the new wringer washer stands ready
mighty fortress against the onslaught of daily life.

Warm sudsy water fills the drum
and a gentle rotation sucks the curtains
into the water until, guided by her expert hands,
the dusty residue of the last few months
of family life is released—
the kitchen fumes, the heated arguments
the fraying promises, all released into the water
until the delicate fabric is rinsed clean and intact.
Then she dips the curtains into a blue pail
filled with her homemade starchy water.

Outside the old fashioned stretcher
erected in the back yard awaits the curtains—
a spindly, adjustable frame of basswood
with tiny silver pins about an inch apart
along the ruler-like edges
where the curtains will be impaled

two or three layers at a time
and the frame stretched by turning the knob
until every last wrinkle disappears
and any stubborn marks are bleached away.

Was it curtains, or was it something more
she was striving for all those years—
every panel, stretched to the hilt
on the wobbly wooden frame
drying in the afternoon sun?

A lacy desire to make this life more perfect
a sheer fear of the future as it stretched before us—
there she is, always and forever,
taking down the billowing curtains
then stretching them to the heavens.

Light Hauling

"Light Hauling," read the ad.
We called and he came quick.
The garage was heaping with

years of assorted junk. Broken-
down chairs, loads of ripped-out rug,
boards with rusty nails.

He backed his red pick-up
to the open garage door
and began the loading.

Hammer in hand,
he flattened everything
he could, slammed it

onto the floorbed of
his truck. He sawed
dad's boards in two and tore

mom's spindly rocking
chair apart with his bare hands.
He made three trips before

he swept the cement floor
clean of dirt and dust,
then leaned upon the broom

and smoked a cigarette.
I'm sixty-nine he said.
My wife just died last month.

The garage lay bare before
us. His squinting blue eyes
asked how we liked his work.

Looks great, we said,
thanked him for his labor
and offered him a beer.

Don't drink no more,
'preciate it just the same, he said
smiling. We paid him cash.

Time and Material
or The Carpenter's Lament

He wears baggy bib overalls,
    work boots and denim jackets

builds decks, garages and sometimes
    even houses too

charging time and material
    instead of the more profitable bid.

"You never charge enough,"
    his wife calls out to him

time and time again. But hard
    of hearing, he leaves the house

oblivious, eyes fixed on his black pickup
    waiting in the icy driveway.

He guns the sputtering engine
    on these bitter winter mornings

skids off and leaves the house
    in a wake of words and blue exhaust.

What could their children know
    sound asleep and dreaming

in their warm beds upstairs
    of the harsh winds waiting below?

Already on the job again
    the driven nails and whining skill saw

Speak the only language that he knows
    and he hums while he hammers the

Knotty boards in place and raises the rafters high
    knocking out another morning cold.

Visits Over Time

Up and down the hilly lawn
I ran among the mossy monuments
playing tag with concrete crosses

kissing ancient angels forever
scattering petals over weeds
and faded plastic flowers until

tired and out of breath I found
my father by the grey granite stone
bearing my grandmother's name—

her name, exactly the same as mine.
Together we would bow our heads
and say a prayer, rain or shine.

Then time came to plant the pungent
red geraniums we carried to her graveside
using tools from the trunk of the Chevy.

He, with his handy trowel, dug up
the loamy earth until dark holes were
ready for watering from his milk bottle.

He shook the plants out of their pots
tamped them down in muddy pools
and coaxed the sturdy, leafy stems upright.

Finally, I took the glass milk bottle
and trickled water all over the nodding
red blooms until the last sandy drop.

Today the smell of geraniums
carries me back to that cemetery,
to the earth he dug and watered

in front of his mother's grave—
to the cloudy sky that loomed above
and the rituals I knew so well.

And now, whenever I visit his grave
I plant a row of imaginary red geraniums
and raise his milk bottle to the sky.

The Last Lesson

The last lesson
mother taught
was how to die.

As with so many
other lessons
she made it seem like

such a natural
thing to do.
When first she

took to bed
it hardly seemed as if
she would spend

her remaining days
there; the late summer
sun dropping kerchiefs

of light around her
seemed to promise quick
recovery, but then

the spells grew more
insistent, the visits
to the hospital grew

more frequent
and the blood transfusions
more urgent

until there was nothing
left. She had taken
flight before us

lifting from her linens
with the grace
of a bird,

her transparent hands
closing 'round the air
of her last day.

Filigree

mother's garden
lay abandoned
in springtime

today her spirit
takes the shape
of a favorite flower

a bouquet
of wilted lilacs
on the kitchen table

a finger of fondness
traces the fallen petals
a keepsake perhaps

for the old album where
family photos lie face to face
in a filigree of family

Baggage

The black pocketbook you carried
the last few years of your life
sits in a corner of my closet
still holding those things
most dear to you—your favorite pen,
your tortoiseshell comb,
your embroidered handkerchief.

Maybe this is the year
I'll discard the purse,
lift every last item from it
until the worn leather hulk
collapses in my grip,
begging me to let it go.

A Host of Voices

The fragrance of honeysuckle around
the house pervades the balmy night
evoking a bygone era of family life
when an immigrant couple married
a century ago and raised eight children.

Now the last grandchild has departed
weeds grow where flowerbeds flourished
paint flakes and peels off wooden trim
windows crack while sills rot
and ivy climbs up dilapidated steps.

Today the bank will auction off
a century of family life in a flash.
A once-favored fig tree abandoned
to the wintry weather shuns this spring
with each bent and brittle branch.

If you walk by late at night
you may hear in the cricket's song
a host of voices from a bygone era
see ghosts dancing with the shadows
in the hazy fragrant moonlight.

His Old Workshop

His old workshop—
only dust and sunlight now
on the wooden counter

Dusk

These are the colors
that break our hearts—

the somber blues and grays
of a rainy day at dusk

this crossing of Nantucket Sound
in late fall.

Whitecaps catch the last glint
of a bruised sun sinking

into the darkening water
while spray leaps up

to the fogged window—
an isinglass on the watery world.

All is mystery now
in the deepening nocturne

of sea and sky, where
each fades into

the other, like the
imperceptible movement

of day into night
summer to winter

or flesh into dust—
your face

already there waiting
in the distant harbor.

Antoinette (Toni) Libro is the author of three previous chapbooks of poetry, *Kokero: Seasons of the Heart* (Horse Press), *Women Without Wings* (with Carol Ann Robertson) (Blackbird Press), and *The House at the Shore and Other Poems* (Lincoln Springs Press).

Her poems have appeared most recently in publications such as the *Adanna Literary Journal; the Aurorean; Paterson Literary Review, Mad Poets Review, Philadelphia Poets, the textbook, The Crafty Poet* and several anthologies. She also writes poetry influenced by an eastern aesthetic, and her haiku and tanka have appeared in *Moonbathing: A Journal of Women's Tanka; Red Lights; The Haiku Calendar 2015* (Snapshot Press, 2014); *Take Five: Best Contemporary Tanka, 2011; Atlas Poetica, Modern Haiku, Frogpond,* and *Prune Juice.*

She is founding editor of *Asphodel: A Literary Journal,* Blackbird Press. She has read at the Geraldine R. Dodge Poetry Festival, the Central Library of Philadelphia, various Barnes and Noble Bookstores, and literary venues throughout the Delaware Valley.

Several of her short stories, some interrelated, have appeared in the *Paterson Literary Review,* with "Welcome Willy," most recently, (Issue 43, 2015-2016), along with her poem, Visits Over Time," which received an Honorable Mention in the Allen Ginsberg Poetry Awards for 2014.

Toni is also a playwright whose plays were produced by Stageworks Touring Company, formerly in residence at Rowan University. Her plays received grants to tour every county in New Jersey and surrounding communities in the Delaware Valley, and for translation into Spanish, such as her trilogy of social realism one-acts: *Out of Bounds, Out of the Shadows,* and *Out of the Cradle.* She is the author of the full-length plays *Dwellers Above the Clouds* and *Watchfire for Freedom*, about the suffragette Alice Paul.

After a teaching career at Rowan University, Glassboro, New Jersey, where she taught for some thirty-five years, Toni retired in 2002, but continued to teach part time, as Professor Emerita, in the Department of English at Rowan University, until recently.

As a frequent participant in literary conferences, Toni attends the Key West Literary Seminar and the Cape Cod Writers Conference on a regular basis, and credits them with providing invaluable instruction, inspiration and encouragement to herself and the writing community. A community arts advocate and consultant, Toni coordinates the Beach Bards Poetry & Prose Reading Series in Sea Isle City, NJ each summer.

She holds a Ph.D. from New York University and continues to write, teach and freelance in New Jersey and St. Augustine, Florida, where she lives with her husband, Louis Braca Jr. and their silver poodle, "Babette." Their daughter, Aimee Lee, and her husband reside in North Jersey.

www.ingramcontent.com/pod-product-compliance
Lightning Source LLC
LaVergne TN
LVHW091235080426
835509LV00009B/1293